Melania Trump Unofficial Memoir

A Must-Read Political Biography of 2025

Carolina Spencer

CBY PRESS

Published by
CBY Press

Ordering Information:
Quantity sales: Special discounts are available on quantity purchases
by corporations, associations, and others.
For details, reach out to the publisher.

First published by CBY Press, 2025

Contents

Author's Note

Dear Reader,

Writing this memoir has been an intimate and reflective experience. My life has brought me in contact with extraordinary events and remarkable people. Along the way, I've experienced moments of great joy and success, but also challenges and heartbreak. Through this book, I hope to reveal the person behind the public image, sharing the values and experiences that have shaped me and offering a glimpse into the complexities of living in the public spotlight. My hope is that my story inspires you, reflecting the universal themes of resilience, love, and the pursuit of dreams.

In a time marked by division and uncertainty, I believe it's important to offer my perspective and share the truth. As someone who values privacy yet has often been subject to public scrutiny and misrepresentation, I feel it is my responsibility to clarify my experiences and set the record straight. By sharing my journey, I hope to foster greater understanding and inspire hope for the future.

Sincerely,

Melania

Chapter 1: USA

"Prepare for landing . . ." the pilot's announcement filled me with excitement as I gazed out the window, hoping to spot New York City. At 26 years old, I had traveled across Europe, but this journey was unlike anything I'd experienced before. This was America–New York–a whole new world.

Deciding to enter the American modeling market had been a careful, deliberate choice. I weighed the risks and rewards bolstered by confidence and my family's support. Leaving behind my life in Europe, I packed my apartment in Paris, met with my agent in Milan, and said emotional goodbyes to my family in Slovenia. With two suitcases and my portfolio–filled with nearly a decade's worth of work–I boarded the plane, determined to make the most of this opportunity.

The flight felt symbolic as if I were moving against the tide–leaving behind familiar European landscapes for a vast unknown. Saying goodbye to my family was tough, but their trust gave me strength. I carried a necklace they gave me, engraved with *Ich liebe dich*–"I love you"–close to my heart as I stepped into the unknown.

When I arrived at JFK Airport on August 27, 1996, I joined the slow-moving visitors' line at immigration. The guards scrutinized each passenger's documents, and I waited patiently, confident in my preparation. When it was my turn, the agent examined me and my passport, asked if it was my first time in the U.S., and then stamped my entry. "Welcome to the United States," he said.

Despite my jet lag, I recognized the significance of the moment. My life had shifted direction, and I felt ready to embrace whatever lay ahead. Outside, the humid air and sounds of traffic greeted me as I waited by the curb. Just when I thought about finding a phone booth, a sleek black limousine pulled up.

"Melania Knauss?" the driver asked.

"Yes. Are you from Metropolitan Models?" I replied.

"Yes, ma'am," he said, opening the door.

I stepped into the elegant interior, grateful to escape the chaos of the airport. As we drove into the city, traffic was heavy, but soon the Manhattan skyline came into view. The Empire State Building, Chrysler Building, and Twin Towers stood tall on the horizon. Seeing these landmarks in person for the first time filled me with exhilaration. Any lingering doubts faded–this was where I was meant to be.

Looking back on that day, I see it as a turning point in my life. Moving to New York symbolized taking full responsibility for my future, a moment when I truly became the architect of my own destiny. Years later, in July 2006, another pivotal moment arrived as I raised my hand, recited the Pledge of Allegiance, and became a U.S. citizen.

The immigration process wasn't easy, but it gave me insight into the challenges faced by others pursuing citizenship. When I finally achieved that milestone, I felt a deep sense of pride and belonging. Becoming an American wasn't just a legal status–it was a personal transformation. I had grown into a citizen of the world, comfortable anywhere, yet now fully at home in the United States.

With gratitude in my heart, I knew that New York wasn't just where my journey began–it was where I was always meant to be.

Chapter 2: The Win

On the morning of November 8, 2016, I woke early to a peaceful, quiet city–calm before the storm. I kissed Barron on the forehead as he slept, knowing the outcome of the day would bring changes none of us could predict. I made a promise to protect him, no matter what lay ahead.

Donald had invested everything in his campaign, building a movement for real change. Now, the American people would decide if they would trust him to lead the country. At 10 a.m., Donald and I left Trump Tower to vote, greeted by crowds of supporters cheering "Trump! Trump!" The energy was electric.

At the polling station, we were met by journalists, election workers, and a few dissenters. I stood beside Donald in the voting booth, overwhelmed with pride, as I saw his name on the ballot. After marking my choices, I took a moment to reflect before we submitted our ballots, completing a small but significant step in the democratic process I had long admired.

We returned to Trump Tower, where we settled in for a long day of waiting. I spent time with Barron and my parents while Donald moved between home and his campaign office, remaining calm and focused. As polls closed at 7 p.m., the media predicted a Hillary Clinton victory, but as the night progressed, the momentum began to shift.

In key battleground states, Donald started gaining ground, defying expectations. By 10 p.m., it was clear the election would not unfold as many had predicted. At 2:30 a.m., the results from Wisconsin confirmed it: Donald Trump had won the presidency. The room erupted in cheers, hugs, and disbelief. We had done it.

Shortly after, we headed to the Hilton Hotel to wait for Hillary Clinton's concession call, which came at 2:40 a.m. Moments later, Donald took the stage to deliver his victory speech, and

Barron and I stood proudly by his side.

“I’ve just received a call from Secretary Clinton,” Donald announced. “Now it’s time for America to bind the wounds of division; we have to get together. I pledge to every citizen that I will be president for all Americans.” His words marked a shift from campaign rhetoric to a message of unity and healing, setting the tone for the work ahead.

Though joy filled the night, my thoughts turned to the responsibilities ahead. Life would change dramatically, especially for Barron, and I knew the transition to the White House would require careful planning. Balancing my roles as mother, wife, First Lady, and daughter would be challenging, especially under media scrutiny. But I was ready to rise to the occasion and help my family navigate this new path.

As the sun began to rise, I finally rested for a couple of hours, reflecting on my journey from a small town far away to standing at the heart of American history. I knew this was only the beginning of a new chapter, and I was ready for the challenges to come.

Chapter 3: April 26, 1970

My mother, Amalija, was born on July 9, 1945, in Judendorf-Straßengel, Austria, where her family had taken refuge during World War II. After the war, they returned to their village of Raka, near Sevnica. My grandfather, Anton, pursued his passion for farming and developed the Raka onion, a sweet red variety beloved in Slovenia. Amalija's creativity led her to study fashion design, and she later worked at the Jutranjka children's clothing factory, where she transformed sketches into patterns. She also instilled in me the importance of self-care, saying, "If I don't take care of myself, how would I know how to care for others?"

My father, Viktor, born on November 23, 1941, in Radee, shared a deep passion for automobiles. His career began in the Yugoslav Army as a driver and progressed to chauffeuring local officials. Eventually, he joined Slovenija Avto as a sales professional and fulfilled his dream of owning a business after Slovenia's independence. My parents married in a civil ceremony at Podvin Castle and later renewed their vows in St. Lawrence Church to honor my mother's Catholic upbringing.

Growing up in Slovenia during Yugoslavia's communist era felt different from other Eastern Bloc countries. Slovenians valued independence, self-reliance, and hard work, and life felt relatively unrestrictive. My hometown of Sevnica, on the banks of the Sava River, provided a beautiful, idyllic setting. Despite the plain exterior of our apartment, my mother's artistic flair transformed it into a vibrant home filled with warmth and creativity.

As a child, I loved playing with Barbies and toy cars, both sparking my imagination. My father's love for cars influenced me deeply, and I cherished our drives together. One of my favorite memories was when he brought home a Citroën Maserati SM. Sitting in the leather back seat as we sped along was thrilling, igniting my lifelong fascination with automobiles.

I was curious and methodical, excelling in school and participating in sports like gymnastics, basketball, and tennis, which my father taught me and my sister Ines. Though I tried playing the guitar, I quickly gave it up when my fingers hurt from the lessons. This experience taught me that while I could do many things, some pursuits were not meant for me.

My sister Ines played a significant role in shaping my love for music and art. We spent nights listening to records and sharing stories, bonding over our creative interests. Some of my fondest memories include attending concerts with her, like Elton John's in 1984 and Tina Turner's in 1990. Traveling with Ines, especially to Venice, introduced me to new cultures and expanded my world.

Summers on the Dalmatian coast were another highlight of my childhood. I can still remember the feel of smooth cobblestone streets under my feet, the taste of gelato, and the sound of music drifting through the air. These experiences filled me with wonder and a sense of freedom, leaving an indelible mark on my heart.

Though life had its challenges, including being teased for my height and appearance, I learned to rise above it with confidence. I realized that these behaviors were often fueled by insecurity, and I refused to let them define me. Reflecting on those experiences, I am grateful that I grew up without the pressures of social media, which amplifies negativity today.

Through these early experiences, I developed a deep appreciation for self-awareness, self-acceptance, and authenticity. My parents' commitment to hard work and creativity laid the foundation for my values, inspiring me to pursue my dreams with determination. Their love and support continue to guide me, and the lessons of my childhood remain central to the person I have become.

Chapter 4: Lights, Camera, Model

At six years old, I experienced my first taste of the fashion world when my mother invited me and my sister, Ines, to model her latest creations in Belgrade. The thrill of stepping onto the runway sparked my love for fashion, and with my mother's encouragement, I joyfully modeled multiple outfits throughout the show. Though I embraced the experience, my focus began to shift from modeling to creating as I grew older, much like my sister.

Inspired by Ines, who attended the Secondary School for Design and Photography in Ljubljana, I also pursued admission and passed the entrance exam, enrolling in industrial design. Living with Ines in Ljubljana gave me both independence and family support as we navigated our academic journeys.

In 1987, my path crossed with photographer Stane Jerko at a fashion show. Though initially unsure of his intentions, I agreed to a photoshoot with him. The session was modest–without professional makeup or styling–but it led to early modeling offers. While I enjoyed these opportunities, I still saw modeling as a hobby, with my primary focus set on becoming an architect.

In 1992, an unexpected second-place win at a modeling competition in Portorož led to an agency contract in Milan. I faced a choice between architecture and modeling, ultimately choosing the latter, knowing I could succeed through determination and hard work. Moving to Milan on my own was intimidating, but I embraced the challenge, navigating castings, photoshoots, and the fast-paced fashion world with resilience.

After two years in Milan, I decided to expand my career and moved to Paris, drawn by the city's reputation for high fashion. In Paris, I worked steadily, focusing on commercial modeling, which suited my physique. During this time, I met Paolo Zampolli, co-owner of Metropolitan Models in New York, who offered me the chance to join his agency. Intrigued, I accepted, ready to explore opportunities in New York.

Arriving in New York, I was captivated by the city's energy. I embraced the challenges of the competitive market, booking jobs with top clients like Bergdorf Goodman and appearing in editorials for Fitness and Glamour magazines. I rented a small apartment near Park Avenue, appreciating the independence it gave me while continuing to explore the city's cultural offerings.

Despite the glamour, the fashion world demanded resilience. Rejections were common, but I never let them discourage me. I stayed focused, avoided distractions, and remained dedicated to my career. Over time, I traveled internationally for prestigious campaigns, building a solid reputation.

Though life in New York was not without challenges, I was motivated by the pride my family had in my achievements. One day, while walking through Midtown, I looked up and saw my image on a Times Square billboard. At that moment, I felt an overwhelming sense of accomplishment, knowing that my hard work and determination had paid off. My journey had taken me from Slovenia to the heart of the global fashion industry, and I had embraced every step with courage and ambition.

Chapter 5:
"Hi, I'm Donald Trump"

In September 1998, a friend invited me to a party at the Kit Kat Klub during Fashion Week. Although tired from a trip to Paris, I agreed. Clubs weren't my favorite, but I welcomed the chance to reconnect with friends and mingle with industry insiders. As we arrived, the club buzzed with energy, filled with models, designers, and photographers. In the VIP section, I noticed a man approaching our table.

"Hi, I'm Donald Trump," he said, extending his hand. I recognized the name but knew little about him. We chatted about my life in New York, my Slovenian roots, and my travels. Though he was accompanied by a date, his focus on our conversation captivated me. His charm and curiosity were refreshing amid the noisy crowd. Before leaving, he asked for my number. I declined but asked for his. He handed me a card with two handwritten numbers and urged me to call.

A few days later, after returning from a photoshoot in the Caribbean, I found his card and decided to call. He returned my call that same night, and we had an easy, engaging conversation. Donald invited me for a drive to Bedford, New York, the following weekend. That Sunday, he picked me up in a black Mercedes, and we spent the day touring his property and talking about life, work, and dreams. I admired his passion for business and his authenticity, finding him unlike anyone I had met.

As we continued seeing each other discreetly, I found joy in our quiet moments, away from the spotlight. Donald's zest for life and his grounded personality were magnetic. Over time, our relationship became public, drawing media attention. The gossip columns speculated about our age difference and accused me of being a "gold digger," but I paid no mind. I had my own career and success long before meeting Donald, and our connection was genuine.

By 2004, we had built a happy life together. I had moved into

Trump Tower, and we spent our time attending events, traveling, and enjoying each other's company. On my birthday in April, just before the Met Gala, Donald surprised me with a stunning diamond ring and proposed. I joyfully accepted, and we began planning our wedding set for January 2005.

Our wedding at Mar-a-Lago was a grand affair attended by family, friends, and celebrities. The day was a celebration of our love, and every detail, from the lavish decor to the exquisite food, reflected our shared taste for beauty and elegance. Following our wedding, I stepped back from modeling to focus on family life. In July 2005, I shared joyful news with Donald: we were expecting a child.

In March 2006, Barron William Trump was born, bringing a new sense of purpose and fulfillment into my life. Motherhood transformed me, teaching me patience, strength, and resilience. I dedicated myself to raising Barron, creating a nurturing home away from the public eye. Donald's love for his son was touching, and our family thrived in the privacy of our shared moments.

In July 2006, I became a naturalized U.S. citizen, a milestone that filled me with pride and a sense of belonging. The journey to citizenship was challenging, requiring perseverance and dedication, but it was a dream come true. Standing with others at the naturalization ceremony, I reflected on the many places I had called home and felt grateful to now be an American. It marked the beginning of a new chapter, one filled with endless possibilities and a future built on love, family, and ambition.

Chapter 6: All Business

By 2009, with Barron in preschool, I had the time to explore new ventures. That year, Marc Beckman from DMA United approached me with the idea of creating a jewelry line. It felt like the perfect opportunity to channel my love for design and fashion. Inspired by a gold bracelet my father gave to my mother, I crafted three distinct collections: Paris (glamorous), New York (business-oriented), and Palm Beach (sporty elegance). The pieces reflected my personal style, designed to be accessible, and priced under $200.

The collection debuted on QVC, selling out within 45 minutes and continuing to break sales records over the next three years. I enjoyed connecting with viewers, offering advice, and receiving compliments on my jewelry. This project symbolized more than fashion; it embodied my passion for independence and empowered other women to pursue their ambitions.

In 2011, I was approached by New Sunshine to create a high-end skincare line. Excited about the venture, I spent months working with chemists to develop products incorporating unique ingredients like caviar. Our collection, including serums, night creams, and exfoliants, was designed to deliver quality results at competitive prices.

Despite promising development, internal disputes within New Sunshine delayed the product launch. After briefly appearing at Lord & Taylor, distribution halted. Frustrated and concerned about my reputation, I took legal action to resolve the breach of contract. The court ruled in my favor, but the experience left me disappointed. I learned valuable lessons about the complexities of business and the importance of aligning with reliable partners.

Though the skincare venture didn't unfold as planned, I remain proud of the products and my efforts. The setbacks did not diminish my entrepreneurial spirit. I look forward to future opportunities to bring new products to market, confident in the lessons I've learned along the way.

Chapter 7: It Is Official

On June 16, 2015, our lives changed forever. From our Trump Tower apartment, I woke early, savoring a final quiet moment before the day's events. My usual routine involved preparing Barron for school, but this day was different. Donald was about to announce his candidacy for president–a step we had carefully planned and discussed for years.

By 10:40 a.m., we gathered in Donald's office with his adult children, the excitement building. I hugged Barron and sent him to the lobby to join the family. Although I hadn't been involved in planning the announcement, I knew my role: Donald and I would descend the escalator, Ivanka would introduce him, and then he would give his speech.

As Donald and I took the elevator to the mezzanine, the atmosphere was electric. Crowds filled the lobby, cheering as we stepped onto the escalator. Those few seconds of descent would become an iconic moment, broadcast around the world. I realized we were entering uncharted territory–our lives were about to change irrevocably.

We joined the family onstage as Donald took the podium. His speech was powerful, direct, and from the heart. He outlined the challenges facing the country–crumbling infrastructure, disappearing jobs, ineffective leadership–and called for a new kind of leader to "make America great again." It was a moment of unfiltered honesty, resonating with many Americans who felt ignored by politicians.

"For the first time, I am officially running for president of the United States," he announced to thunderous applause. Over the next forty-five minutes, Donald laid out his vision with passion and conviction. He spoke not just as a politician but as someone deeply connected to the concerns of everyday Americans.

After the speech, we stood together for photos before returning to our apartment. In the quiet that followed, I reflected on the significance of the moment. Our lives had changed, and the campaign ahead would be demanding. Yet, I felt an overwhelming sense of pride for Donald and gratitude for the journey we had shared since our first meeting years ago.

I knew that serving alongside him in this new role would be both a challenge and an honor—a responsibility I was ready to embrace.

Chapter 8: Why Was the Speech Not Vetted?

After Donald announced his candidacy, the campaign took off, with daily speeches and travel across the country. By May 2016, Donald had secured the Republican nomination, and I was honored to be included in the program for the Republican National Convention. This was my chance to introduce myself to the American public on my own terms, sharing my story and my belief in Donald's leadership.

I was excited but also nervous about addressing such a large audience. After receiving an initial draft of the speech from the campaign, I felt it didn't capture my voice. I wanted to emphasize the values of kindness, compassion, and my personal journey to the United States. With Donald's suggestion, I worked with Meredith McIver, a representative of the Trump Organization, to refine the speech. During our discussions, I referenced speeches by past First Ladies, including one by Michelle Obama, whose words about hard work and kindness resonated with me.

On July 18, 2016, I took the stage at the convention. The audience responded warmly as I spoke about my journey to America and expressed my commitment to helping children and women if given the opportunity to serve as First Lady. I ended with a heartfelt endorsement of Donald, proclaiming him ready to lead the nation.

On the flight home, my sense of accomplishment was shattered by accusations of plagiarism–similarities between my speech and Michelle Obama's speech were discovered. I felt betrayed, wondering how such a critical oversight had happened. I had trusted the campaign and expected the speech to be properly vetted, but now I faced public humiliation. Meredith apologized publicly, explaining that some phrases from Michelle's speech had been mistakenly included. But the damage was done.

The controversy marked a turning point in my relationship with the media. Soon after, nude photos from my early modeling career resurfaced, splashed across the New York Post with salacious headlines. Although I wasn't ashamed of the photos, as they reflected European attitudes toward art and nudity, they were weaponized to hurt Donald's campaign. Misreporting also fueled false rumors that I had worked illegally in the U.S.

The media frenzy worsened when the *Daily Mail* published defamatory claims that I had once worked as an escort. These baseless stories, repeated without any verification, led me to file lawsuits in both the U.K. and U.S. The *Daily Mail* eventually retracted its statements, issued an apology, and paid damages, as did a blogger who had spread similar falsehoods.

This experience was a harsh introduction to the realities of political life and media scrutiny. I realized I could no longer trust others to protect my reputation–I had to take control of it myself. I also became even more determined to shield Barron from the relentless public spotlight. Despite the challenges, I knew the scrutiny would only intensify if Donald won the presidency, and I prepared myself for what lay ahead.

Chapter 9: On My Way

Earlier, when asked what kind of First Lady I would be, I answered that I wanted to be traditional, like Jackie Kenn. However, by the time Donald's campaign became a reality in 2015, I understood that being a First Lady in the modern era would require a unique approach. With today's media and constant internet exposure, the carefully controlled image Jackie Kennedy maintained seemed impossible. My goal was to serve with authenticity, dignity, and strength while embracing both tradition and the reality of a divided nation and hostile media.

Being the first foreign-born First Lady in centuries presented its challenges, and I knew that not everyone would welcome me with open arms. The political landscape had already tested friendships, but I decided to surround myself with genuine, supportive people, focusing on unity regardless of political affiliations. My aim was to serve all Americans with respect and fairness.

The morning after Donald's election victory, life shifted into high gear. There was no time for reflection as we prepared to travel to Washington for our first official duties as President- and First Lady-elect. The schedule was relentless, and the transition began immediately. As we boarded Donald's 757, the airport ground crew honored us with a ceremonial water salute, marking the beginning of this new chapter for our family and the nation.

Our first stop in Washington was the White House, where the Obamas warmly welcomed us. Michelle offered me a tour, and we shared tea in the Yellow Oval Room. She answered my questions with kindness, and despite media expectations of tension, our meeting was pleasant and constructive. Michelle's advice about life in the White House, especially raising a young child like Barron, was invaluable.

Upon returning to New York, I focused on building my team for the First Lady's office. The transition team provided me with a detailed agenda and a chart listing over twenty positions to fill. Building a team from scratch felt like running a large corporation, but I embraced the responsibility, determined to assemble a staff that could serve the nation effectively.

While managing the transition, I also prepared for our family's move to Washington and the inauguration. My primary advocacy focus would be children's well-being and cybersecurity–issues I had long cared about and now had the platform to champion. Balancing these responsibilities with Barron's daily needs was a challenge, but I was determined to ensure stability for him amid the changes.

Looking forward to the future, I felt ready to embrace my role as First Lady. I knew it wouldn't be easy, but I was confident in my ability to inspire others by balancing family, leadership, and advocacy. With each step forward, I was motivated to serve the American people and meet the challenges of this new chapter with resilience and grace.

Chapter 10:
My Husband,the President

On January 19, 2017, we arrived at Joint Base Andrews, our final flight as president- and First Lady-elect behind us. The next day, Donald would officially become president. While Donald attended a leadership luncheon, Barron and I checked into Blair House, the President's Guest House, a tradition we were honored to uphold. The day was filled with ceremonies, including a solemn wreath-laying at Arlington National Cemetery.

Later, Donald addressed supporters at the Lincoln Memorial, promising: "I'll see you tomorrow... What we've done is so special." As the crowd cheered, the gravity of the moment sank in—it was truly the beginning of a new chapter for our family and the country.

On Inauguration Day, I woke early to a whirlwind of preparations. I wore a custom Ralph Lauren blue ensemble—a dress, matching jacket, gloves, and Manolo Blahnik heels—understanding it would become a part of history. The day began with a prayer service at St. John's Episcopal Church, followed by a visit to the White House where we exchanged gifts with the Obamas.

At the Capitol, I stood with Barron and my parents as Donald took the oath of office, his hand on two Bibles—one from his childhood and the other used by Abraham Lincoln. When Chief Justice John Roberts declared, "Congratulations," and the band played "Hail to the Chief," I knew our lives had changed forever.

The inauguration ceremony was followed by a lunch at the Capitol, where Donald asked the attendees to give Hillary Clinton a standing ovation in a rare bipartisan moment. We then joined the grand inaugural parade down Pennsylvania Avenue, with eight thousand participants, including military units and bands. Donald and I stepped out of the limo twice to engage with the cheering crowd.

That evening, I changed into an off-white, off-the-shoulder gown designed by Hervé Pierre for the inaugural balls. The dress featured a high slit and a red silk belt, perfectly blending elegance and modernity. At the Liberty and Freedom Balls, Donald and I shared our first dance to "My Way" by Frank Sinatra. We ended the night at the Salute to Our Armed Services Ball, where we spoke via satellite with troops stationed in Afghanistan.

When we finally arrived at the White House late that night, it felt surreal–like staying in a hotel rather than a home. The next morning, we attended the National Prayer Service at the Washington National Cathedral and later celebrated with family in the State Dining Room. January 22 marked our twelfth wedding anniversary, and it felt fitting to reflect on how much had changed in those years.

The inauguration was a monumental event, not just for us but for the nation. Though steeped in tradition, it carried a new energy, with enthusiastic supporters surrounding us. It was the beginning of an exciting, unpredictable adventure–a journey we were eager to embark on together.

Chapter 11: In the White House

Becoming First Lady was often described as the "hardest volunteer job in America"—a highly visible, unpaid role subject to intense scrutiny. However, I saw it as an opportunity to make a positive impact. The role came with responsibilities beyond family duties, including overseeing White House staff, planning events, hosting foreign dignitaries, and responding to unforeseen crises such as national tragedies and disasters.

In early 2017, I split my time between New York, Washington, and Mar-a-Lago, balancing my duties as First Lady while caring for Barron. Establishing my office was challenging, given tight timelines and limited resources. While previous First Ladies managed large teams, I kept my staff small but effective, focused on achieving my goals.

In February, Donald and I hosted Japanese Prime Minister Shinzo Abe and his wife at Mar-a-Lago, followed by my first official speech at a Florida rally. Seeing the support and enthusiasm from the crowd reminded me of the faith people had placed in us.

Preparing for our move to the White House took careful planning. Decorating the residence was complicated by delayed access, which limited my ability to prepare before the inauguration. With the help of interior designer Tham Kannalikham, I worked on creating a comfortable and welcoming space for our family, including redecorating Barron's room to suit his interests. In June 2017, we finally made the move to the White House.

The transition to public life presented challenges, especially for Barron, as we adjusted to increased security and scrutiny. Despite these challenges, the summer move allowed us time to settle before Barron started his new school in September. I remained focused on supporting my husband's work while fostering stability for our family.

Once settled, I prioritized restoring the White House, ensuring it remained both a home and a symbol of American pride. With Tham's help, we redecorated rooms like the Queen's Bedroom and restored the historic Zuber wallpaper in the President's Dining Room. Other renovations included refreshing the Green and Red Rooms, upgrading the curators' area, and restoring the East Room floor.

In 2018, I also undertook the design of a new White House Tennis Pavilion, working closely with architects and historians to create a structure in harmony with the White House's classical style. Despite criticism for continuing the project during the pandemic, many workers expressed gratitude for the opportunity to keep their businesses running.

Another major project was the renovation of Camp David. We updated the facilities while preserving the retreat's rustic charm, ensuring it remained both functional and historically authentic.

My work on the Rose Garden was a particular point of pride. We made essential upgrades, including improved accessibility and irrigation, while adding "Floor Frame," a sculpture by Isamu Noguchi, to honor resilience and renewal.

Through these projects, I aimed to preserve the White House's legacy while ensuring it remained beautiful and functional for future generations. These efforts—undertaken quietly, away from political noise—were my way of contributing something lasting to the American people.

Chapter 12:
Welcome to the White House

Hosting events at the White House was one of the most demanding yet rewarding aspects of my role as First Lady. From state dinners to the annual Easter Egg Roll, every event required meticulous planning to ensure perfection.

Our first major event was the Governors Ball in late February 2017. Working with designer David Monn, we embraced the theme of "Spring's Renewal" to foster unity among the guests, which included governors from both political parties. As cohosts, Donald and I welcomed guests in the Blue Room, and the State Dining Room's elegant decor made the evening a success, setting the tone for future bipartisan collaborations.

Throughout the year, my schedule was filled with meaningful events. On Valentine's Day, I visited the children at the National Institutes of Health (NIH) hospital, sharing crafts and treats with them. In March, I hosted a luncheon for International Women's Day and later spoke at the International Women of Courage Award Ceremony. Hearing the inspiring stories of women standing up against forced marriages and violence reaffirmed my commitment to supporting global causes.

State dinners were formal affairs that demanded special attention. For our first state dinner with French President Emmanuel Macron and his wife, Brigitte, I took a hands-on approach, personally overseeing every detail. Brigitte and I developed a warm friendship, which made hosting the dinner even more special. To honor the occasion, I wore a custom silver Chanel gown. Every element of the evening, from the French-inspired music and cuisine to the carefully selected guest list, symbolized the enduring friendship between France and the United States.

Christmas at the White House was another cherished tradition. Planning for the holiday season began as early as July. Volunteers from across the nation helped decorate the residence, and the festivities kicked off with the arrival of the official Christmas tree just before Thanksgiving. After returning from Mar-a-Lago, Donald and I welcomed guests to view the decorations. It was a joyful season, with events bringing together military families, Secret Service members, and government officials, celebrating the spirit of community and gratitude.

Chapter 13: Be Best

In a speech in Berwyn, Pennsylvania, just days before Donald's election, I shared my concerns about the dangers children face in a world dominated by technology and social media. I stressed the importance of teaching respect, empathy, and kindness, especially in the digital age. The internet, though powerful, has become a breeding ground for bullying and harmful behavior, and children are often left to navigate these challenges without guidance or protection.

The impact of online bullying hit home when Rosie O'Donnell publicly questioned whether Barron had autism, sharing a video that scrutinized his behavior. This cruel act devastated me as a mother. Though O'Donnell later apologized, the damage was done. Barron's experience highlighted the toxic effects of cyberbullying, inspiring me to address this growing issue through my platform as First Lady.

In 2017, I hosted a luncheon at the United Nations, emphasizing the need to teach empathy and promote online safety. Later, I met with major tech companies, including Facebook and Twitter, to discuss how they could help protect children from online harassment. However, I encountered resistance from executives, who cited free speech concerns. Despite this, I remained committed, encouraged by the support of parents across the country who shared their own struggles with me.

On May 7, 2018, I launched *Be Best*, an initiative with three main pillars: children's well-being, online safety, and combating opioid abuse. In the Rose Garden speech announcing the program, I stressed the importance of equipping children with tools to navigate the digital landscape responsibly. Donald joined me to express his pride and officially declare May 7 *Be Best Day*.

Though some critics mocked the program's name, I stood by it. The phrase "Be Best" symbolized confidence and positivity, resonating with the initiative's goals. International leaders, including Brigitte Macron and Queen Mathilde of Belgium, expressed their admiration and sought to launch similar programs in their countries.

A key focus of *Be Best* was addressing the opioid crisis. I hosted a roundtable at the White House to hear stories from families affected by addiction and visited Lily's Place in West Virginia, where I witnessed the heartbreaking effects of opioid withdrawal on newborns. These experiences deepened my commitment to advocating for solutions.

By 2019, *Be Best* had gained momentum, particularly in advancing online safety measures. My discussions with Microsoft executives led to progress in implementing parental controls on platforms like Xbox. The initiative's work on the opioid crisis also expanded, helping families and raising awareness of neonatal abstinence syndrome.

Be Best aimed to spark conversations and drive meaningful change for the benefit of children. While the challenges were immense, I was proud of the program's impact in promoting online safety, addressing opioid addiction, and encouraging leaders worldwide to prioritize the well-being of children.

Chapter 14: Going Global

In May 2017, our first major international trip took us to Saudi Arabia, Israel, Rome, Belgium, and Sicily. The trip required meticulous planning by the State Department, West Wing, and East Wing. I was excited to visit schools and hospitals during our stops, as these connections with local communities were a priority for me.

Our journey began in Saudi Arabia, where we were warmly welcomed by King Salman, who greeted me with a handshake and kiss—breaking tradition. The visit showcased the region's hospitality, and I was impressed by the professionalism of women working at General Electric's all-women center, a rare sight in the country.

In Israel, we were welcomed by Prime Minister Benjamin Netanyahu and his wife, Sara. Despite media fabrications about an innocent hand gesture between Donald and me, I focused on meaningful experiences, including visiting children at Hadassah Medical Center with Sara. We also explored cultural sites, such as the Western Wall and the Church of the Holy Sepulchre.

Our next stop was Rome, where I met Pope Francis and received a blessing for my rosary, a meaningful moment as a Catholic. We visited Bambino Gesù Children's Hospital, where I met a young boy awaiting a heart transplant. Miraculously, we later learned on our flight to Belgium that a heart had been found for him.

In Belgium, Queen Mathilde and I discussed online bullying and shared ideas on how to protect children online. The trip concluded in Sicily, where we attended the G7 summit and engaged with other leaders.

Later that year, I traveled to China, where I toured a local school with Madame Peng and participated in cultural activities. I was impressed by the discipline and respect shown by students.

These moments reminded me of the importance of education and tradition in building strong communities.

In 2018, I embarked on my first solo trip as First Lady to Africa, visiting Ghana, Malawi, Kenya, and Egypt. In Ghana, I laid a wreath at the Door of No Return, a powerful reminder of the history of slavery. In Malawi, I visited overcrowded schools, distributing supplies and books. In Kenya, I had the joy of feeding baby elephants at a wildlife orphanage. Finally, in Egypt, I marveled at the Pyramids and met with the country's leaders.

A memorable moment came during a surprise Christmas visit to troops stationed in Iraq. Flying under the cover of darkness, we arrived at Al-Asad Airbase, bringing holiday cheer to the soldiers. Our visit underscored the importance of showing gratitude for their service.

Our travels continued with a visit to Japan, where we met Prime Minister Abe and his wife, Akie. I admired their kindness and enjoyed seeing Be Best-inspired artwork created by children. We also attended a sumo wrestling tournament, where Donald awarded the champion a trophy.

Our final stop was in the UK, where we shared memorable moments with Queen Elizabeth II at Buckingham Palace. The Queen's warmth left a lasting impression, and our connection with the Royal Family continues to this day.

These global experiences were not just diplomatic events; they were opportunities to engage with different cultures, support children, and honor our troops. They shaped my understanding of the world and deepened my commitment to making a positive impact through my role as First Lady.

Chapter 15: Moments of Crisis

The role of the First Lady demands readiness for unpredictable crises. In August 2017, when Hurricane Harvey devastated Texas and Louisiana, Donald and I quickly traveled to offer support. On the ground, we met victims and relief workers, ensuring resources were provided. One encounter with a woman who lost everything stands out–her resilience reminded me of the strength that emerges from tragedy.

A month later, on October 1, 2017, a mass shooting in Las Vegas left 60 people dead and hundreds wounded. Visiting victims in the hospital, we witnessed incredible strength. One injured man insisted on standing to greet us despite his pain. The resilience of the American people was a recurring theme during my tenure as First Lady.

In June 2018, immigration policies that separated families at the U.S.-Mexico border sparked outrage. I was deeply concerned and immediately discussed the issue with Donald, urging him to stop the separations. He responded by signing an executive order ending the policy, but I felt compelled to visit the border myself. My first trip to a children's center in Texas confirmed the importance of family reunification, and my second trip to Arizona reinforced my commitment to ensuring children's well-being despite the challenges.

One moment that drew significant media attention was my choice to wear a jacket with the message "I really don't care, do you?" upon returning from Texas. The media misinterpreted it, claiming it reflected a lack of concern for the children. In truth, it was aimed at the media itself, expressing my frustration with their distorted narratives.

In late 2019, I accompanied Donald to the Situation Room to witness a mission to eliminate ISIS leader Abu Bakr al-Baghdadi. Observing the bravery and precision of the U.S. special forces during the operation was a humbling experience. The mission's success was later celebrated with a visit to the White House by Conan, the Belgian Malinois military dog who played a vital role in the raid.

Throughout these crises, my goal as First Lady was to offer compassion and support to those in need, navigating both personal and national challenges with empathy and resilience.

Chapter 16: 2020

As Barron approached his 14th birthday, I marveled at the intelligent, charming, and diligent young man he had become. Navigating life under the spotlight with confidence, Barron continued to amaze me with his maturity and resilience through the whirlwind of his father's presidency.

On June 18, 2019, we officially launched Donald's reelection campaign in Orlando, Florida. Addressing the crowd, I expressed pride in our family's work and excitement for another term. Despite opposition, Donald's speech highlighted economic successes and challenges he had overcome, including impeachment. The impeachment, driven by political opposition, ended with the Senate acquitting Donald.

In December 2019, news of a novel coronavirus emerged from China. Donald took swift action, implementing a travel ban from China in January 2020, which likely saved lives. As COVID-19 spread, the White House adapted quickly, closing offices and implementing health protocols. In the midst of this crisis, we also traveled to India for a planned state visit with Prime Minister Modi. The trip went smoothly, but it marked the end of international travel during Donald's presidency.

As COVID-19 cases surged, I organized public service announcements and distributed Be Best supplies to hospitals and shelters. I wanted to offer a sense of calm and gratitude for frontline workers. The situation escalated with protests following the killing of George Floyd in May 2020. While peaceful protests are essential, I expressed concern over the violence and destruction that spread across cities.

Tensions increased when protests reached the White House in late May. On May 29, the Secret Service evacuated us to the bunker as rioters threatened the gates. Though I initially resisted, Donald remained calm, respecting the security team's decisions. After a tense two hours, we returned to the residence, reflecting on the challenges ahead.

The campaign continued amid these crises, but on October 1, Donald and I tested positive for COVID-19. While my symptoms were mild, Donald's were more severe, leading to his brief hospitalization at Walter Reed. We recovered, though the experience reminded us of the virus's unpredictability. Barron also tested positive but experienced no serious symptoms.

Election night arrived with suspense, as early wins turned into delays due to mail-in voting. As the results dragged on, it became clear Donald's path to victory was uncertain. On November 7, the media called the election for Joe Biden, bringing disappointment but also a sense of acceptance. I focused on preparing for our move to Mar-a-Lago and finding a new school for Barron.

On January 6, 2021, as Congress certified the election, I was working on archival documentation in the White House. I was unaware of the unfolding events at the Capitol until I received a message asking if I wanted to denounce the violence. Confused, I later learned about the riot and immediately condemned the violence, recognizing the importance of peaceful protest and unity in moving forward.

Chapter 17: Fostering the Future

On January 20, 2021, Donald and I left the White House, saying emotional farewells to our staff. As Marine One lifted off, I reflected on the honor of serving as First Lady and prepared to embrace the future. Landing at Mar-a-Lago, I realized my work would not stop; I was determined to make a difference beyond the White House.

Shortly after our transition, I began developing "Fostering the Future," an initiative under the Be Best umbrella focused on supporting children in foster care. I had learned that many foster children lacked stability, education, and career opportunities. The statistics were sobering: only half graduated high school, and only 3% earned a college degree. With "Fostering the Future," I aimed to provide scholarships for foster children to pursue tech-focused education, empowering them to achieve financial independence and a brighter future.

The program also reflected my interest in blockchain technologies. To fund it, I launched digital platforms, including collectible ornaments and jewelry, using blockchain for greater autonomy and direct engagement with supporters. Despite challenges, such as partners canceling contracts due to political pressures, I remained committed to the program's success.

Our early efforts faced hurdles, including the withdrawal of a tech-education partner after political backlash. This experience underscored the prevalence of cancel culture, which extended beyond social media into the corporate world. I encountered situations where potential collaborators distanced themselves for fear of backlash, leaving foster children—those the initiatives aimed to help—as the true victims. Despite these challenges, we found new partners and continued to push forward, determined to make a lasting impact.

I reflected on my core belief in individual liberty—the fundamental right for people to make personal decisions about their lives.

This belief extends to issues like women's health, emphasizing autonomy in making choices about pregnancies. I have always advocated for common-sense policies, recognizing that personal freedom lies at the heart of a dignified life.

In August 2022, the FBI's raid on Mar-a-Lago shocked me deeply. While in New York for a medical appointment, I received a message from my house manager about agents surrounding our home. Watching the media coverage, I felt violated–our personal space had been invaded without warning. Learning that agents had searched my bedroom and even Barron's room filled me with anger and disbelief. It was a grim reminder of the abuses I witnessed growing up under Slovenia's communist regime, where government overreach was a reality.

This experience reinforced my belief in protecting individual rights from government intrusion. Watching a similar violation occur in my adopted country was disheartening. Americans must stay vigilant to ensure such abuses do not become the norm, safeguarding their freedoms before they are lost.

Though no longer First Lady, my commitment to fostering the future endures. I continue advocating for vulnerable children and promoting freedom, using every tool at my disposal to build a safer, more hopeful tomorrow.

Chapter 18
"Good Luck and Be Safe"

It had been a relatively quiet Saturday in Bedminster. Barron played sports outside. I was working on finishing my project. Around 6 p.m., I turned on the TV to watch Donald's speech but paused it after five minutes. I needed a brief moment of uninterrupted focus to complete my tasks before resuming the rally.

"Are you watching the rally?" My chief of staff said when I picked up, her voice shaky. "Yes, I have it on," I said, "but I paused it. What's going on?"

"I just want to let you know he's okay. He . . . is . . . okay," she said slowly. "But there was a shooting."

I rushed to the TV and pressed play. I couldn't believe what I was seeing. Standing transfixed in front of the television, I watched the chaos unfold: the gunfire, Donald instinctively reaching up to his head, and the immediate response of Secret Service agents shielding him. Though my chief of staff insisted Donald was unharmed, the footage suggested otherwise.

"He's on the ground," I called out. "Are you sure he's okay?"

"I was told he is," she reassured me. "He's on the way to the hospital, but he's fine."

My mind racing, I hung up and immediately dialed Donald. When he didn't answer, I contacted his Secret Service detail. Thankfully, they told me they were already at the hospital and, after what felt like an eternity, put Donald on the line. "I'm okay," he assured me. It was only when I heard his voice that I could finally believe that he really was fine.

Now, Barron rushed in, his faced filled with worry.

“What happened? Is Dad okay?” he asked, breathlessly.

The Secret Service had told him there had been an incident at the rally and that he should go inside.

“He is okay,” I told him.

Barron wanted to see what was happening, so we replayed the footage and watched it together. We were both in shock. As we tuned into the news coverage, I felt a deep sense of distress. Can I explain how traumatic it is for a child to witness the attempted murder of his father? The relentless replay of the rally footage on the news only intensified our anxiety. Each time we saw Donald’s bloodied face, I had to remind myself that I had actually just spoken to him, heard his voice, and knew that he was safe.

Before Donald announced his first candidacy in 2016, we had talked about the implications of his decision on his and our personal safety. We recognized the inherent risks associated with such a high-profile position, including the potential risk to him, to me, and, hardest to contemplate, even to Barron. We have come to terms with these realities, but the worry never goes away.

As a wife and mother, the safety of my family is a constant concern. Before Donald’s arrival in Pennsylvania for the rally, I reminded him, as I always do before his public appearances, “Good luck and be safe. I’ll be watching.”

Donald was discharged from the hospital after an observation period and returned home to Bedminster at 2 o’clock in the morning. Barron and I felt relieved at seeing him and hugged him.

The next morning, we discussed the Republican National

Convention in Milwaukee and the concerns about safety. Donald was adamant in his decision to attend, determined to confront any potential threats. Donald possesses an innate ability to see the positive side of situations. He always stays focused on the fight ahead. The violence he had just experienced actually reinforced his dedication to lead the country toward stability and progress. Within just a few hours, he was on his way to Milwaukee.

In the days that followed that harrowing and surreal event, I found myself reflecting on the sequence of moments that led to my husband's near-tragic brush with fate. Donald's survival that day was nothing short of a miracle. Without a rapid shift to his right in his movement, the shooter's aim would have led to a horrible and tragic outcome.

Reflecting on the multitude of possible scenarios made me consider the fragility of life, and I am grateful that he returned safely to his family that night.

Life is precious and can be lost in an instant. At the rally, attended by thousands, that attempted assassination of my husband claimed the life of a brave firefighter named Corey Comperatore, who shielded his wife and two daughters from the bullets with his body. Two other men sustained serious injuries.

Our nation stands at a pivotal moment. We have a choice: to be torn apart by violence, hatred, and division, or to unite in a spirit of love, kindness, and shared humanity. It is critical that we choose the latter before it is too late.

On the morning of July 14, 2024, I drafted a letter to the American people, the kind of letter I had hoped would never be necessary.

I am thinking of you now, my fellow Americans.

We have always been a unique union. America, the fabric of our gentle nation is tattered, but our courage and common sense must ascend and bring us back together as one. When I watched that violent bullet strike my husband, Donald, I realized my life, and Barron's life, were on the brink of devastating change. I am grateful to the brave Secret Service agents and law enforcement officials who risked their own lives to protect my husband. To the families of the innocent victims who are now suffering from this heinous act, I humbly offer my sincerest sympathy. Your need to summon your inner strength for such a terrible reason saddens me.

A monster who recognized my husband as an inhuman political machine attempted to wring out Donald's passion–his laughter, ingenuity, love of music, and inspiration. The core facets of my husband's life–his human side–were buried below the political machine. Donald, the generous and caring man who I have been with through the best of times and the worst of times.

Let us not forget that differing opinions, policy, and political games are inferior to love. Our personal, structural, and life commitment–until death–is at serious risk. Political concepts are simple when compared to us, human beings.

We are all humans, and fundamentally, instinctively, we want to help one another. American politics are only one vehicle that can uplift our communities. Love, compassion, kindness and empathy are necessities.

And let us remember that when the time comes to look beyond the left and the right, beyond the red and the blue, we all come from families with the passion to fight for a better life together, while we are here, in this earthly realm.

Dawn is here again. Let us reunite. Now.

This morning, ascend above the hate, the vitriol, and the simpleminded ideas that ignite violence. We all want a world where respect is paramount, family is first, and love transcends. We can realize this world again. Each of us must demand to get it back. We must insist that respect fills the cornerstone of our relationships again.

I am thinking of you, my fellow Americans.

The winds of change have arrived. For those of you who cry in support, I thank you. I commend those of you who have reached out beyond the political divide—thank you for remembering that every single politician is a man or a woman with a loving family.

Sincerely,

Melania Trump